INCREDIBLE EDIBLE SCIENCE

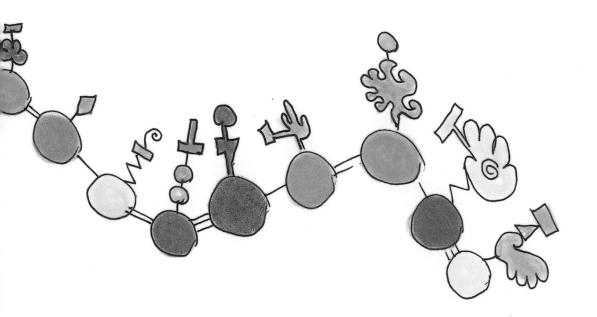

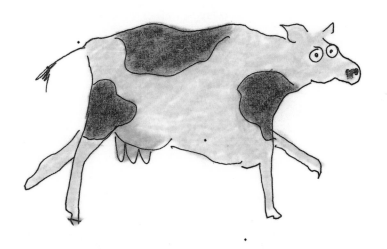

**For my son, Josh,
whom I love more than chocolate**

—*T. L. S.*

Scientific American Books for Young Readers is an imprint of
W. H. Freeman and Company,
41 Madison Avenue, New York, New York 10010.

Book design by Debora Smith

Library of Congress Cataloging–in–Publication Data

Seelig, Tina Lynn.
Incredible edible science/ Tina L. Seelig; illustrations by Lynn Brunelle. Includes index.
ISBN 0–7167–6501–2 (hard). — ISBN 0–7167–6507–1 (soft)
1. Cookery—Juvenile literature. 2. Food—Juvenile literature.
[1. Cookery. 2. Food.] I. Brunelle, Lynn, ill. II. Title.
TX652.5.S42 1994
641.5—dc20

93–33480
CIP
AC

Printed in the United States of America
10 9 8 7 6 5 4 3 2 1

Note: Neither the publisher nor the author shall be liable for any damage that may be caused or any injury sustained as a result of doing any of the recipes or other activities in this book.

INCREDIBLE EDIBLE SCIENCE

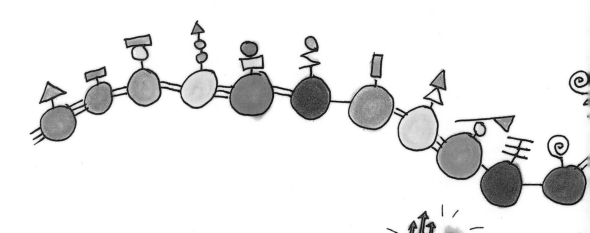

Tina L. Seelig

illustrations by Lynn Brunelle

Scientific
BOOKS FOR YOUNG READERS
American

W. H. FREEMAN   NEW YORK

CONTENTS

CONTENTS

INTRODUCTION

Have you ever thought of your kitchen as a chemistry laboratory? They may look very different but when you cook, you use many of the same methods that chemists use in a laboratory.

Both cooks and lab scientists measure and combine ingredients. They both heat, cool, shake, and stir their mixtures. They both keep careful track of all the steps they take—the recipe—so that they can repeat the steps later. And when they see changes that have occurred in their ingredients, they both ask, "How did that happen?"

Have you ever wondered why onions make you cry when you cut them? Why oil and water don't mix? Why popcorn pops? These cooking mysteries and many others have puzzled people for years. But science can answer these questions—and so can you!

Each section of this book asks a question about cooking that you may have wondered. It leads you through a scientific investigation to find the answer. And it finishes with a delicious recipe that demonstrates some of the scientific principles at work. Take the time to think about the scientific principles. Try the recipes. Then experiment with recipes of your own, based on your new understanding.

Remember:

- *Like a chemistry laboratory, a kitchen can be a dangerous place. Obey all safety rules.*

- *Unless you are an experienced cook and have permission to use the kitchen, get an adult to help you use the stove, the oven, or any dangerous cooking utensil. Use ovenproof mitts or pot holders whenever you handle hot objects.*

- *If you don't understand a term, look it up in the glossary at the back of the book.*

- *And, finally, don't forget to clean up!*

COOKING UTENSILS

At the top of each recipe you'll find little drawings like these that show you what cooking utensils you need.

Frying pan (skillet)

Cutting board

Jar with lid

Measuring cups

Saucepan (pot)

Sieve

Electric mixer or hand beater

Knife

Fork

Slotted spoon

Bowl

Pastry brush

Stirring spoon

Measuring spoons

Skewers

Wire rack

Rolling pin

Deep fat/candy thermometer

Container with lid

Square pan (8- or 9-inch)

Oven thermometer

Muffin tin

Pizza pan

Thermos

Baking sheet

Cheesecloth

7

SOLUTIONS

When you cook, chemical reactions take place. Most of these chemical reactions occur in solutions. What is a solution? It is a mixture of ingredients in which one or more ingredients dissolves—breaks up—in a liquid.

Try adding a teaspoon of table salt to a cup of water. If you stir the water, the salt disappears. Where does it go? The salt has dissolved. It has formed a chemical relationship with the water. This means they won't separate on their own. The easiest way to separate them is to boil away the water, changing it into a gas and leaving the salt behind.

But not all ingredients dissolve in all liquids. Try adding a teaspoon of flour to a cup of water. Does the flour dissolve? No. This is because flour particles do not form a chemical relationship with the water. However, they are suspended— held up—by the water molecules for a short time. This kind of mixture is called a suspension. Eventually, the flour will fall down to the bottom of the cup.

Finally, try adding a teaspoon of oil to a cup of water. What happens? They quickly separate because oil and water are so different that they cannot be mixed. The oil rises to the top of the cup.

In this section you will discover some useful things about solutions:

- *Why a liquid boils.*

- *How its boiling point can be changed.*

- *How you can change the freezing point of a solution.*

- *What the difference is between fat and oil.*

- *How you can trick oil and water into mixing.*

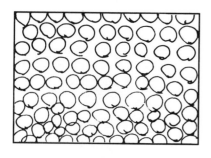

Solid

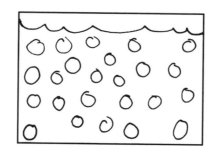

Liquid

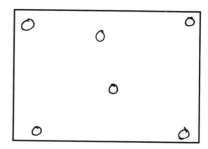

Gas

Quick Chemistry

All matter (everything that has weight and takes up space) is made up of about 100 substances called elements. All elements are made up of tiny atoms, which are far too small to be seen even under a microscope. The atoms in an element join together to form longer units called molecules.

Sometimes atoms join together with atoms of another element and form a kind of molecule called a compound. This is an entirely new substance. For example, two atoms of the element hydrogen and one atom of the element oxygen make up a molecule of water. Sugar is made up of several carbon, hydrogen, and oxygen atoms. Some molecules are made up of hundreds of atoms.

Matter can be found in three different states: solid, liquid, and gas. Particles in a solid are strongly attracted to one another, so they don't move around much. A solid has a definite shape and volume (amount of space it takes up). Particles in a liquid are less strongly attracted, so they move and slide over one another. A liquid has no definite shape, but its volumes stays the same. Gas particles are only weakly attracted to one another, so they spread out to fill any size container they're in.

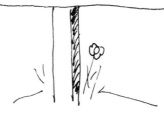

Why does water boil?

Have you ever heard the saying "A watched pot never boils"? Well, a watched pot *always* boils—if it reaches a high enough temperature. But what is boiling and why does it happen?

A single teaspoon of water is made up of billions of water molecules that are constantly moving. Some move so fast that they evaporate—bounce out of the liquid and enter the air as water vapor, a gas. This goes on all the time, but you can't see it. If left long enough, all the water in the teaspoon will evaporate.

The water molecules that evaporate push upward on the air above the teaspoon. This is called the vapor pressure. The air above the teaspoon pushes down on the water. This is called the atmospheric pressure because it is the weight of all the air directly above the teaspoon.

When you heat a pot of water on the stove, the water molecules move faster and faster. The hotter the water, the faster they escape into the air. When the water is pushing up-ward as hard as the air is pushing back, the water boils. The water bubbles and swirls and even makes noise.

The boiling temperature of water at sea level is 212°F (100°C). No matter how much you heat the water, it can't get hotter than its boiling point. Cooking food in rapidly boiling water does not cook food any faster than cooking it at a low boil. It just causes the water to boil away more quickly. That's why many recipes tell you to turn the heat down to a simmer after the liquid boils—to keep it at the boiling point without boiling away all the liquid.

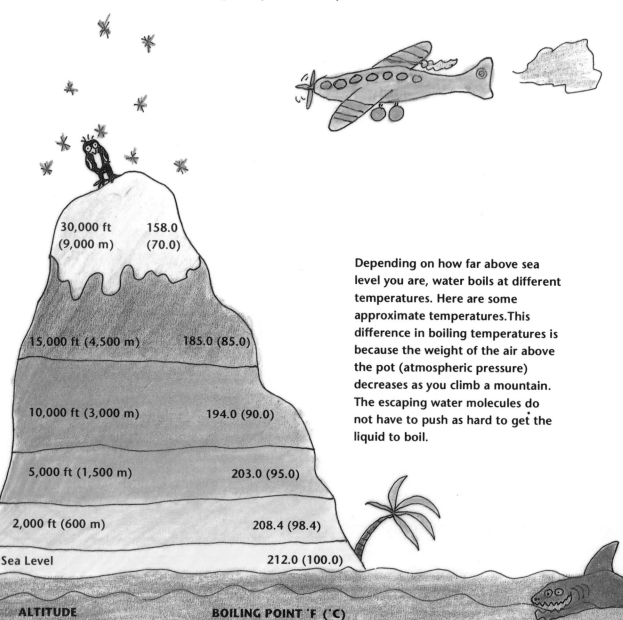

Depending on how far above sea level you are, water boils at different temperatures. Here are some approximate temperatures. This difference in boiling temperatures is because the weight of the air above the pot (atmospheric pressure) decreases as you climb a mountain. The escaping water molecules do not have to push as hard to get the liquid to boil.

ALTITUDE	BOILING POINT °F (°C)
30,000 ft (9,000 m)	158.0 (70.0)
15,000 ft (4,500 m)	185.0 (85.0)
10,000 ft (3,000 m)	194.0 (90.0)
5,000 ft (1,500 m)	203.0 (95.0)
2,000 ft (600 m)	208.4 (98.4)
Sea Level	212.0 (100.0)

Different liquids boil at different temperatures. The temperature at which a liquid boils depends on how strong the bonds (links) are between the atoms and between the molecules in the liquid.

SUBSTANCE	BOILING POINT °F (°C) at sea level	
Iodine (antiseptic for cuts)	363.8	(184.4)
Water	212.0	(100.0)
Rubbing Alcohol	180.3	(82.4)
Propane (fuel for grills)	−43.8	(−42.1)

WARNING: Do not try to boil any of these liquids except water!

You can cook many different kinds of foods, such as eggs, vegetables, and grains, in boiling liquid. People all over the world cook grains to eat as hot cereal, a side dish, a main course, or even dessert. In all of these dishes, the grain absorbs the boiling liquid. Here are some delicious recipes.

2 cups water

2 tablespoons butter or margarine

1/2 teaspoon salt

1 cup couscous

3/4 cup raisins

1 teaspoon cinnamon

Surprising Cereal—Couscous

This delicious grain (pronounced KOOSS-kooss), a specialty of North Africa, is made from semolina, a kind of wheat. This recipe is for hot breakfast cereal, something like Cream of Wheat. With a few changes it can become a side dish at dinner or a dessert. Many supermarkets carry couscous. If you don't find it at yours, try a health food store.

1. In a heavy saucepan, bring the water, the butter, and the salt to a boil.

2. Gradually add the couscous, stirring with a wooden spoon.

3. Continue to boil and stir for about 2 minutes, until the water is almost absorbed.

4. Stir in the raisins and the cinnamon, remove from heat, cover tightly, and let stand for 10 minutes.

5. Fluff with the wooden spoon and dish the couscous into cereal bowls.

6. Serve with milk. Add a little extra salt and some sugar if you want.

Makes 4 servings.

For side dish: If you think the sweet taste will not go with your main course, prepare the couscous as above but don't add the milk, sugar, raisins, and cinnamon. Increase salt to 1 teaspoon. Makes 4 to 6 servings.

For dessert: Prepare as in original recipe. Spoon into 6 dessert dishes. Don't add milk, but sprinkle with cinnamon and more sugar, if you like. Top with whipped cream. Makes 6 servings.

If you'd rather go with the tried and true, here are other suggestions for cooking grains in boiling water.

Oatmeal: Not the so-called instant kind that comes in packets, but the kind you measure out yourself. Follow manufacturer's directions. Then dress it up with your favorite extras—fresh fruit, raisins, brown sugar and cinnamon, honey and almonds, or maple syrup.

Rice: Prepare according to package directions. Store 3 cups cooked rice in the refrigerator until the next day, for the Fancy Fried Rice recipe in this book. Or for a different breakfast treat, spoon into cereal bowls and add raisins, sprinkle with 1/4 teaspoon cinnamon, pour in milk, and add sugar to taste.

How do you make ice cream?

"I scream, you scream, we all scream for ice cream!" Almost everyone loves ice cream. It is a mixture of a few simple ingredients: cream, sugar, and flavoring. But if you just toss them together and put them in the freezer, you don't get the rich taste and firm but light texture. What's the secret?

Three things have to happen when you make ice cream:

- *The water in the cream must freeze solid into tiny ice crystals. The crystals make the ice cream firm.*

- *The mixture must be whipped in order to mix in tiny air bubbles. The bubbles make the ice cream light.*

- *The fat in the cream must coat the ice crystals and the air bubbles. The fat makes the ice cream rich and creamy.*

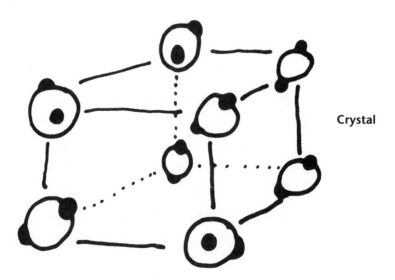

Crystal

When water freezes, it forms regular patterns called ice crystals.

The most important thing to know about making ice cream is that when you dissolve the sugar in the cream, it lowers the temperature at which the water in the cream freezes—forms ice crystals—below its usual freezing temperature of 32°F (0°C). The more sugar in the mixture, the lower the freezing point. In order to make the ice cream freeze, you have to lower the temperature of the mixture. How do you do that?

For years, home ice-cream makers have been available. The oldest kind has three main parts:

- *An inner canister into which the mixture of cream and sugar is placed.*

- *A paddle (or dasher) inside the canister that turns, in order to whip air into the ice cream and to break the forming ice into tiny crystals. The paddles always used to be turned by hand, but now most are turned electrically.*

- *An outer canister that holds the ice and rock salt, which chill the inner canister.*

Why is salt added to the ice? Because the salt lowers the freezing point of water. The ice melts and the cold water mixes with the salt, forming brine—salty water—that can get much colder than plain water before it freezes. It makes the ice-cream mixture in the canister get colder and colder—until the ice cream freezes.

In recent years, another kind of ice-cream maker has been used too. The freezer contains an alcohol solution instead of salt and ice in its outer canister. The ice-cream maker is placed in the freezer in order to freeze the alcohol solution. Since alcohol freezes at a lower temperature than water, the outer canister is cold enough to freeze the ice cream. Then the paddle method is used to whip the ice cream

Even if you don't have an ice-cream maker, you can still make ice cream—as long as you have a freezer and set it at its coldest setting. By beating some of the ingredients together until they get very fluffy, more air gets into the mixture. You don't use a paddle to mix in air. Although the results may not be quite as good, you will still have a delicious treat. This is called still-frozen ice cream. So if you don't have an ice-cream maker, follow the special directions for still-frozen ice cream at the end of the recipe.

People have been enjoying ice-cream–like desserts for 4,000 years. In China, a favorite food of the rich was milk ice. It was made from a soft paste of rice, spices, and milk, which was then packed in snow. Ice cream traveled to Europe in the 1300s and to the United States with Thomas Jefferson around 1800.

Chocolate-Chip Ice Cream

Ice-cream-maker version

1. In a small saucepan, beat together the eggs, milk, sugar, and salt until well blended.

2. Cook, stirring constantly, over very low heat, until the mixture thickens enough to coat a metal spoon.

3. Cool completely in the refrigerator.

4. Stir in the heavy cream, vanilla, and chocolate chips.

5. Chill in the refrigerator for at least 2 hours.

6. Turn the mixture into the metal canister of an ice-cream maker and freeze according to the manufacturer's directions.

7. Remove the dasher and scoop the ice cream into a 1-quart container. Cover and place in the freezer for 2 to 5 hours. This will make the ice cream harder and allow the flavors to blend.

Makes about 1 quart.

2 eggs

1 cup milk

1/2 cup sugar

1/8 teaspoon salt

1 1/2 cups heavy cream

2 teaspoons vanilla

1/2 cup semi-sweet mini chocolate chips

Still-frozen method

Cook and cool the mixture as in steps 1 to 3 on page 19. In a large bowl, use a mixer to beat the heavy cream and vanilla until stiff peaks form. (To test, turn off the mixer. The cream should hold its shape when the beaters are lifted out of the bowl.) Do not overbeat the cream, or you will make butter. Gently fold the egg mixture into the whipped cream until it is well blended. Gently fold in the chocolate chips. Turn into a 1-quart container. Cover and place in the freezer until the ice cream is firm, about 4 hours. This ice cream will not be as smooth as the ice-cream-maker version.

Mint Chocolate-Chip Ice Cream

Prepare the ice cream as above, substituting 1 teaspoon mint extract for the vanilla. Add 4 drops of green food coloring, if desired, with the extract.

What is the difference between fat and oil?

Fat, such as that found on meat, and oil, such as corn or olive oil, are very similar. They are made of the same kind of molecules — but fats are solid at room temperature and oils are liquid. The size and shape of the molecules determines if they are solid or liquid.

Some fat molecules are long and straight, and others are short and bent. The long, straight molecules (saturated fats) stack together easily and form a solid fat. The short, bent fat molecules (unsaturated fats) don't stack easily and are usually liquid at room temperature.

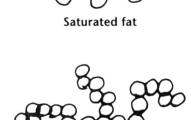

Saturated fat

Unsaturated fat

Saturated Fats The carbon atoms in these fat molecules are "saturated" with hydrogen atoms. This means they have as much hydrogen bound to them as possible. The resulting molecule is straight.

Unsaturated Fats The carbon atoms in these fat molecules are "not saturated" with hydrogen. This means there is less hydrogen than possible. The resulting molecule is bent wherever it is missing hydrogen atoms.

HEY, FATTY!

Animals and plants store fat as an energy supply. Animals store fat throughout their bodies to use when food is scarce. Plants store fat in their seeds to provide fuel for sprouting.

21

Fancy Fried Rice

2 strips of bacon

1/4 cup peanut or other vegetable oil

1/2 cup chopped onion

2 cloves garlic, chopped or crushed

1 teaspoon freshly grated ginger or 1/4 to 1/2 teaspoon ground ginger

1/2 cup thin-sliced carrots

1 cup quartered and sliced zucchini

1/2 cup fresh or thawed frozen peas

2 eggs, lightly beaten

3 cups cooked rice, preferably one day old

1/4 cup soy sauce

1. In a large frying pan or wok, fry the bacon until the heat changes the fat to liquid and the meat is brown and crisp. Remove the bacon and drain it on paper towels, leaving the bacon drippings in the pan. When the bacon cools, crumble it into small pieces and set aside.

2. Add the peanut oil, onions, garlic, and ginger to the hot bacon drippings. Cook and stir over medium heat until the onions are soft and slightly browned.

3. Add the sliced carrots. Cook and stir until the carrots soften. Add the zucchini and cook and stir until it softens. Add the peas and cook only until they are heated through. Turn off burner. Remove the vegetables from the pan with a slotted spoon and place them in a large bowl.

4. Over medium heat, add the beaten eggs to the hot drippings. Scramble the eggs until they are well cooked. Break them up with the slotted spoon and add them to the bowl with the vegetables.

5. Add the rice to the pan with the hot drippings. Cook and stir until hot. Add the soy sauce and mix well.

6. Add the crumbled bacon and the vegetable-egg mixture to the hot rice. Cook and stir until heated through. Serve immediately.

Makes 4 to 6 servings.

Why don't oil and water mix?

Both oil and water are used in many sauces and salad dressings. You can shake a jar of oil and water from today to tomorrow, but when you stop, they will separate. Why?

It's all in the molecules. Water is made up of polar molecules, which are like magnets. Just as the negative end (pole) of one magnet is attracted to the positive end (pole) of another magnet, the negative side of a polar molecule is attracted to the positive side of another polar molecule.

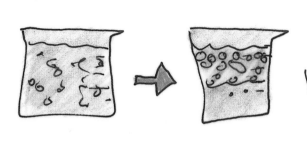

But oil is not made of polar molecules. So instead of attracting the polar water, it is pushed away. But in which direction? Since oil is lighter than water, it naturally rises to the surface.

It is possible to get oil and water to mix by using a third substance that acts as a "peacemaker." The molecules in the peacemaker, called emulsifiers, have two ends, or "hands." One "hand" is water-loving and grabs hold of a water molecule. The other "hand" is water-fearing and grabs hold of an oil molecule. In this way the emulsifier becomes a bridge between the water and the oil.

Common cooking emulsifiers include egg yolk, mustard, yogurt, honey, and dried herbs. Egg yolks are used in making mayonnaise. Mustard is used in making vinaigrette salad dressing.

Oil

Emulsifiers

Water

Here is a delicious recipe for salad dressing. See what happens when you combine the vinegar and the oil. Then add the mustard and watch it all come together.

Honey-Mustard Salad Dressing

2 tablespoons cider vinegar

2 tablespoons vegetable oil

1 tablespoon honey

1 tablespoon Dijon-style mustard

Salt and pepper to taste

1. Place vinegar and oil in a small jar with a tight lid.

2. Shake well and see what happens.

3. Add honey and mustard and shake. See the difference?

4. Add salt and pepper to taste. Shake before pouring over your favorite salad vegetables.

Makes about 1/3 cup.

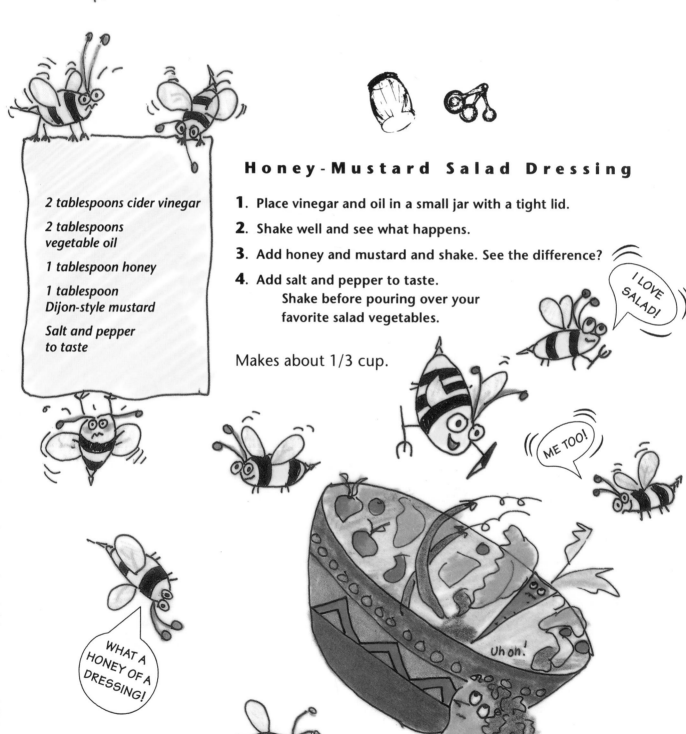

24

ACIDS AND BASES

Did you know that you eat acids and bases all the time? You eat an acid whenever you chomp on a pickle or sip hot chocolate. You eat a base whenever you bite into the white part of an egg. In fact, all foods can be described as acidic, basic, or neutral. Knowing the differences can tell you a lot about how ingredients will react with each other.

You can tell how acidic or basic some foods are by tasting them. For example, vinegar and lemon juice, which are both quite acidic, are sour. Water is neutral and has no strong taste unless strong-tasting chemicals, used to keep germs out, are added. Baking soda, which is basic, tastes bitter.

The amount of acid or base in a substance can be measured on a special scale called pH. The scale goes from 1 to 14, with 7 as neutral. The more acidic the substance, the lower the number on the pH scale. The more basic the substance, the higher the number on the pH scale. (Another word often used for *basic* is *alkaline*.) When acids and bases are mixed together in the right amounts, they can neutralize each other.

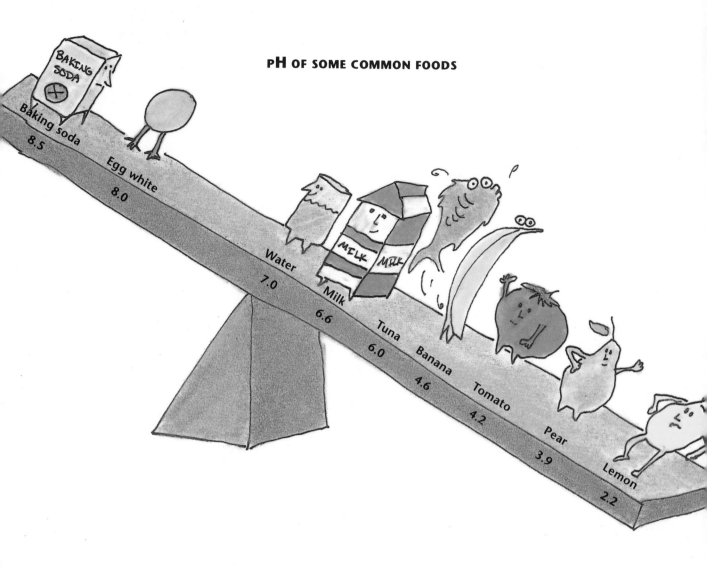

pH OF SOME COMMON FOODS

Baking soda 8.5

Egg white 8.0

Water 7.0

Milk 6.6

Tuna 6.0

Banana 4.6

Tomato 4.2

Pear 3.9

Lemon 2.2

In highly acidic solutions proteins change shape, and long sugars such as starch break apart into small pieces.

In the following sections you will see how acids or bases:

- *Help batter rise.*

- *Prevent cut fruits from browning.*

- *Turn cucumbers into pickles.*

What is the difference between baking soda and powder?

When you make cakes, muffins, or biscuits, the recipes always call for baking soda or baking powder. If you try to make these recipes without baking soda or baking powder, you will probably end up with an inedible mess. Why? Because they make your batter rise. But they are used under different conditions. What are those conditions?

Baking soda is a base. It is used in batters containing acidic liquid ingredients such as lemon juice, buttermilk, yogurt, sour cream, pineapple juice, molasses, melted chocolate, and vinegar. The baking soda and the acid react chemically, neutralizing each other and releasing carbon dioxide gas. The gas is trapped as bubbles in the batter.

When the batter is placed in a hot oven, the bubbles expand. The batter expands around them, making it rise. Cut a muffin in half and look at all the little holes. They were formed by this process, which is called leavening. The baking soda is known as the leavening agent.

If baking soda is used in a batter that is not acidic enough, there will not be enough carbon dioxide bubbles to make the batter rise. The baking soda that hasn't reacted with acid makes the batter taste very bitter.

How do you get your batter to rise if it doesn't contain much acid? You can use baking powder. Baking powder contains baking soda *plus* an acid. When baking powder is added to liquid ingredients, the baking soda in it reacts with the acid, and bubbles form. These bubbles expand in the oven, and the batter rises.

Some recipes call for both baking soda and baking powder. In these cases, there is probably some acid in the recipe but not enough to leaven the batter fully. Baking powder is needed in addition to baking soda to get the correct amount of leavening. After the batter is baked and removed from the oven, the carbon dioxide bubbles escape into the air. You are left with a delicately light cake, muffin, or biscuit. There should be no remaining bitter-tasting baking soda or baking powder.

I'M OUTTA HERE!

Buttermilk Raisin Muffins

1. Preheat the oven to 400°F (200°C).

2. Grease a muffin tin or place a paper liner in each muffin cup.

3. In a large bowl, mix thoroughly the flour, baking powder, cinnamon, baking soda, and salt.

4. In another bowl, mix together the buttermilk, egg, and oil.

5. Pour the wet ingredients into the dry ingredients and mix them only until the dry ingredients are moistened.

6. Stir in the raisins.

7. Spoon the batter into the prepared muffin tin.

8. Bake for 20 minutes, or until the muffins are slightly browned on the top and a toothpick inserted in the center of a muffin comes out clean.

9. Take the tin from the oven. Remove the muffins and let them cool on a wire rack. Serve warm or cool.

Makes 12 muffins.

2 cups flour

2 teaspoons baking powder

1 teaspoon cinnamon

1/2 teaspoon baking soda

1/2 teaspoon salt

1 cup buttermilk (the acid)

1 egg

1/4 cup vegetable oil

2/3 cup raisins

Why does cut fruit turn brown?

If you've ever bitten or cut into an apple, a pear, or a banana and then left it sitting around for a while, you've probably noticed that the fruit turns brown. Inside every fruit are pigment molecules that give it its color. When you cut open the fruit, these molecules are exposed to the air and start to turn brown.

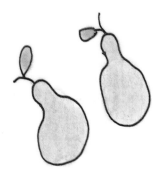

Some kinds of fruit—apples, bananas, pears—turn brown more quickly than others—oranges, grapefruit, melons. That's because the first three have a special enzyme, a type of molecule that speeds up the browning. But this enzyme can be damaged, and the browning can be slowed down.

For example, if you cut apples and bake them in a pie, the oven's heat destroys the enzyme and stops the apples from turning brown. Or if you put sliced apples in the refrigerator, the cool temperature slows down the enzyme and the browning. Other ways to slow the enzyme—and the browning—include adding salt or acid to the fruit. Since highly salted fruit doesn't taste very good, most people add an acid such as lemon or orange juice to cut-up fruit to keep it looking fresh.

Summer Fruit Salad

1. In a large bowl, combine the peaches, pears, bananas, strawberries, and grapes.

2. Sprinkle the fruit with the orange juice.

3. Toss gently to mix well.

4. Sprinkle with coconut.

5. Refrigerate until ready to serve.

Makes 8 servings.

2 peaches, cut in bite-size pieces

2 pears, cut in bite-size pieces

2 bananas, sliced

1 cup strawberries, halved

1 cup grapes

1/4 cup orange juice

1/4 cup flaked coconut

If you want to make this fruit salad during a season when you can't find fresh peaches, use apples. If you can't find fresh strawberries, thaw frozen ones. Or combine your favorite fruits, keeping the total amount of fruit about equal to that in the recipe.

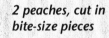

Why are pickles sour?

Pickles are cucumbers that have been treated so they can be eaten long after they are picked. There are sour pickles, and there are sweet pickles. But even sweet pickles are not entirely sweet—they're sweet and sour. There's a good reason why pickles are sour—they *need* to be. Why?

Almost all the food that you eat is also food for tiny living things called microbes that you can see only under a microscope. These microbes include bacteria, yeast, and molds. In most cases, they cause food to rot, making it taste bad. In some cases, such as cheese and yogurt, special microbes added to the food make the food what it is and give it its special taste.

Drying: When you dry fruit such as apricots or apples, you remove the water so that microbes cannot survive.

Pickling: When you add an acid such as vinegar or lemon juice to vegetables, the acid kills the microbes and allows you to store the vegetables for a longer time without spoiling. The acid gives the food a sour taste.

Freezing: When you freeze food, you slow down the growth of microbes so much that the food does not spoil as quickly.

Most microbes are fairly delicate and cannot live in places without enough water or where there is a lot of acid, sugar, heat, or cold. You can, therefore, slow down the growth of microbes by changing their environment.

Preserving, drying, salting, canning, freezing, and pickling are methods that allow us to enjoy all winter long the foods that we grow during the summer.

Canning: When you can fruits and vegetables, you heat them to a high temperature in the can to kill any unwanted microbes that would cause the produce to spoil.

Preserving: When you make jam, you add a large amount of sugar to the fruit. This draws water out of the microbes and kills them.

MICROBES BEWARE!

HELP!

Salting: When you make beef jerky, you add so much salt to the meat that water is drawn out of it. The microbes cannot live because water is no longer available.

Pickles are made by adding a mixture of vinegar, salt, sugar, and spices to cucumbers. You can also pickle other vegetables, such as green tomatoes, onions, peppers, mushrooms, and cauliflower. Here is a quick pickle recipe that's actually more like a Swedish cucumber salad than the pickles you get from a jar that require long pickling.

Puckered Pickles

1. In a large bowl or plastic container with a watertight lid, mix the vinegar, water, sugar, dill, and salt until the sugar and salt dissolve.

2. Add the cucumbers and onion. Mix well. Add pepper, if you like.

3. Cover the mixture and refrigerate it for at least 2 hours, stirring occasionally. (If the mixture is in a plastic container, turn the container over occasionally to mix the ingredients.)

Makes 6 to 8 servings.

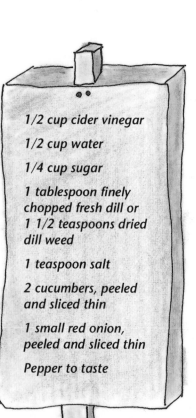

1/2 cup cider vinegar

1/2 cup water

1/4 cup sugar

1 tablespoon finely chopped fresh dill or 1 1/2 teaspoons dried dill weed

1 teaspoon salt

2 cucumbers, peeled and sliced thin

1 small red onion, peeled and sliced thin

Pepper to taste

SUGARS AND STARCHES

Do you have a sweet tooth? Most people do. It has been passed down, generation to generation, since prehistoric times. Before people grew their own food, their ability to taste sweetness helped them tell whether a plant was good or bad. Most plants that taste sweet are ripe and nutritious. Unripe and poisonous plants are usually bitter. Although we no longer need a sweet tooth to tell the difference between good and bad food, we are left with our love for sugar.

Plants make sugar through photosynthesis—a process by which they capture the energy from sunlight. They produce sugar to store energy and to build new plant cells. Plants store sugar in the form of starch, which is a long chain of sugar molecules. Seeds, such as corn kernels and rice, contain a lot of starch. The starch serves as the fuel that the seeds use for sprouting. Sugar molecules in plants can also form cellulose, which makes up the firm structure that holds plants together.

You use many different sugars and starches when you cook. In the following sections you will see how:

- *You can use concentrated sugar solutions to make candy.*

- *Starch thickens a sauce.*

- *The starch inside corn kernels explodes to make popcorn.*

How do you make candy from sugar?

Hard candy is made from sugar—the same granulated sugar that's in your sugar bowl. But how do you get hard, colored, glossy, solid candy from tiny white grains?

To make lollipops, for example, you need a syrup that is almost all sugar with just a tiny bit of water—1 to 2 percent—to keep it liquid. To make such a solution, mix the sugar and water together in a heavy pot until all the sugar dissolves. Then you boil away almost all the water.

How do you know when you reach 98 or 99 percent sugar? There are two ways to tell. One is by looking at the boiling temperature, as measured on a candy thermometer. The higher the sugar concentration, the higher the boiling temperature. The other method is by observing what happens when a small amount of the mixture is placed in ice water.

Temperature °F (°C)	Percent Sugar	Test Results
230 (110)	70%	Spins thread when dropped into ice water.
240 (116)	80%	Forms soft ball when dropped into ice water.
255 (124)	90%	Forms hard ball when dropped into ice water.
300 (149)	98-99%	Forms hard ball that cracks when dropped into ice water.

From the chart you can see that your lollipop mixture is ready when a small amount of it reaches 300°F (149°C) on the candy thermometer or forms a hard ball in the ice water.

$$CHO$$
$$H - C - H$$
$$HO - C - H$$
$$H - C - OH$$
$$H - C - OH$$
$$C\ H_2\ OH$$

C is a carbon atom.
H is a hydrogen atom.
O is an oxygen atom.

Sugar molecule

If you boil away a lot of the water and then cool the solution, it becomes supersaturated. This means it has more sugar in it than can stay in solution. Crystals of table sugar begin to form. Some candy, such as fudge, gets its texture from the formation of many tiny crystals. Rock candy forms when large crystals grow slowly. When making lollipops, you want to avoid crystallization, which gives lollipops a grainy texture.

There are two ways to avoid crystallization. One is to cool the mixture very quickly, so there is less time for the crystals to form. A second way is to add corn syrup to the table-sugar solution. Corn syrup is made of several different types of sugar molecules, with different shapes. They prevent the molecules of table sugar from stacking together into crystals.

In the lollipop recipe that follows, you will be doubly insured against crystallization by mixing corn syrup into your solution *and* by spooning the mixture into small portions, allowing the lollipops to cool quickly.

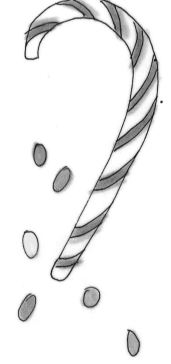

Loony Lollipops

Caution: Be extremely careful when working with hot sugar solution. It's even hotter than boiling water.

1/2 cup light corn syrup

1/2 cup water

1 cup sugar

1 teaspoon vanilla

4 drops red food coloring

Lollipop sticks, or wooden skewers cut in half

1. Line 3 baking sheets with aluminum foil. Place the lollipop sticks or wooden skewer halves on foil, about 3 inches apart.

2. In a 1-quart saucepan, mix the corn syrup, water, and sugar. Cook over high heat, stirring with a wooden spoon, until the mixture comes to a full boil. If sugar crystals form on the sides of the pan, wash them down with a pastry brush that has been dipped in water.

3. Boil the mixture until a candy/deep-fry thermometer registers 300°F (149°C), or until a small amount of syrup placed in a cup of ice water forms a hard ball that cracks.

4. Remove the pan from the heat. Stir in the vanilla and the food coloring. The vanilla will bubble when added to the hot syrup.

5. Carefully spoon the very hot mixture onto the lollipop sticks, making sure that the syrup covers the top inch or two of the stick.

6. The lollipops will be cool in about 20 minutes. Carefully peel them from the foil by gently lifting the sticks.

Makes about 24 two-inch lollipops.

What makes pudding and gravy lumpy?

Have you ever had a delicious turkey dinner with cran-berries and sweet potatoes—and gravy with horrible little lumps in it? Gravies, sauces, and puddings get lumpy because their ingredients—starch, fat, and water—are added in the wrong order. The starch is what makes them thick, and it is also what causes lumps if used incorrectly. The most common starches used in cooking are cornstarch, potato starch, wheat flour, rice flour, tapioca, and arrowroot.

If you are making gravy, it is important to add the starch, usually wheat flour, to hot fat drippings or cool liquid. That way the bits of starch, called granules, get mixed evenly through the drippings. They can't clump together when added to the rest of the liquid.

Pudding can also get lumpy. Maybe you always eat pudding from plastic containers or from a mix. Then you may never have seen lumpy pudding. But when it is made from separate ingredients, it can turn out thin and lumpy. How does this happen? How can you prevent it?

If you add dry starch directly to hot water or milk (milk is mostly water), the starch granules become sticky on the out-side and stay dry on the inside. The sticky granules lump together. These lumps, with raw starch on the inside, don't ever break up. They look strange and taste strange. And the rest of the pudding is thin.

Starch granules

Starch lump

But if you add starch to cold liquid, the individual starch granules are evenly dispersed, absorb the liquid, and swell like sponges. They don't get a chance to get lumpy. As you heat the mixture, even more liquid gets absorbed, and the pudding gets thicker.

As the pudding cools, starch molecules that have leaked out of the starch granules create a large net that keeps the liquid in the pudding from moving around. Your pudding then becomes thick and creamy.

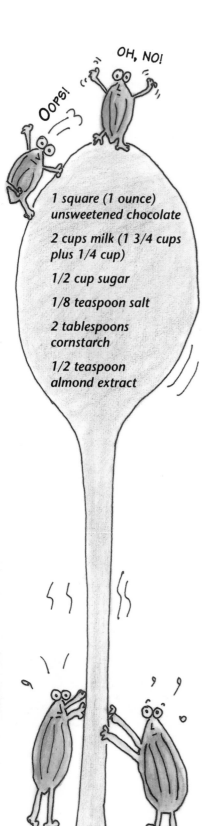

1 square (1 ounce) unsweetened chocolate

2 cups milk (1 3/4 cups plus 1/4 cup)

1/2 cup sugar

1/8 teaspoon salt

2 tablespoons cornstarch

1/2 teaspoon almond extract

Chocolate-Almond Pudding

1. In a 2-quart saucepan, combine the chocolate, 1 3/4 cups of the milk, the sugar, and the salt.

2. Cook and stir over medium heat until the milk is very hot but not boiling. The chocolate will not be completely melted.

3. In a small bowl, mix the cornstarch and the remaining 1/4 cup of milk until the cornstarch is completely dissolved.

4. Stir the cornstarch mixture into the hot milk. Cook over low heat, stirring constantly, until the mixture comes to a boil.

5. Boil and stir for 1 minute. (The chocolate should be completely melted.)

6. Remove from heat. Stir in the almond extract.

7. Pour the pudding into 4 individual custard cups or into a serving bowl.

8. Refrigerate for several hours, until the pudding sets.

Makes 4 servings.

Note: If you prefer, use 1 teaspoon vanilla instead of the almond extract.

Why does popcorn pop?

Can you think of any other food that changes as quickly as popcorn when it is cooked? Popcorn starts out as small, hard, golden kernels. In a split second it turns into light, fluffy, white or yellow puffs. How does that happen?

Corn contains water, protein, and starch. But not all corn pops, as Native Americans living at least 5,000 years ago discovered. That's because different types of corn contain different amounts of water, protein, and starch. They are used for different purposes, such as popcorn, corn oil, corn flour, for animal feed, and so on.

The corn used to make popcorn normally contains about 16 percent water when fresh. In order to make it pop, it is dried so that it contains between 13 and 14 percent water. After the popcorn has been dried, it is sealed in airtight containers to prevent the corn from absorbing water.

When you make popcorn, you must heat the kernels to a very high temperature in hot oil or by surrounding them with hot air in an air popper or a fireplace. Both oil and air can be heated to temperatures much higher than boiling water, which turns to steam at 212°F (100°C).

Popcorn kernel

**Popcorn kernel
with water heating inside**

**Popcorn kernel
popped**

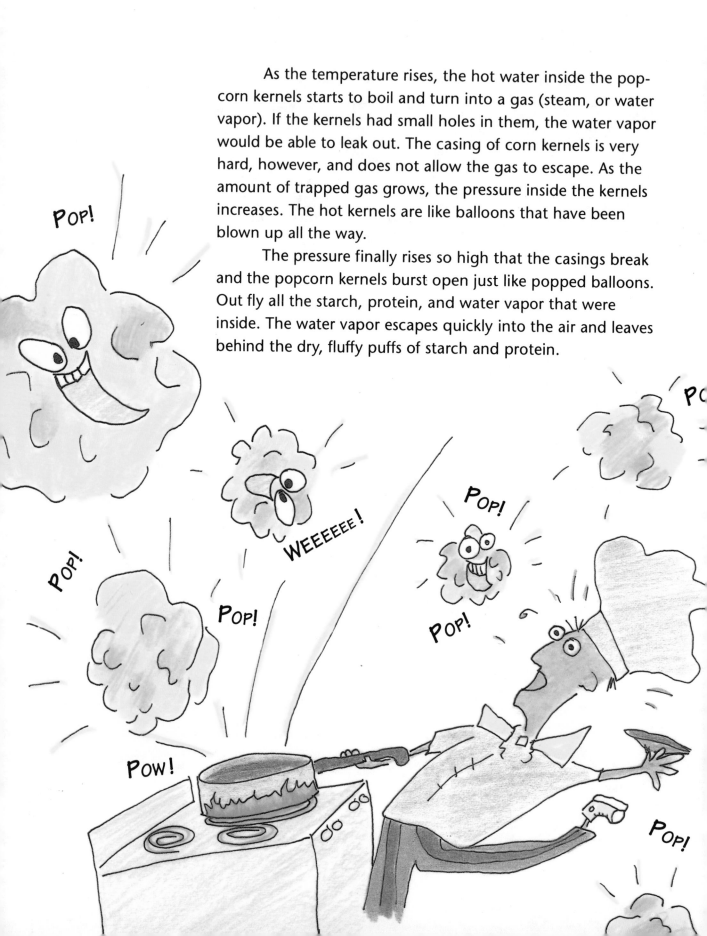

As the temperature rises, the hot water inside the popcorn kernels starts to boil and turn into a gas (steam, or water vapor). If the kernels had small holes in them, the water vapor would be able to leak out. The casing of corn kernels is very hard, however, and does not allow the gas to escape. As the amount of trapped gas grows, the pressure inside the kernels increases. The hot kernels are like balloons that have been blown up all the way.

The pressure finally rises so high that the casings break and the popcorn kernels burst open just like popped balloons. Out fly all the starch, protein, and water vapor that were inside. The water vapor escapes quickly into the air and leaves behind the dry, fluffy puffs of starch and protein.

Freshly made popcorn left in a covered pot will quickly reabsorb the water vapor and become soggy. So it's important to pour freshly made popcorn into an open bowl and eat it!

Popcorn Nachos

1. Follow the manufacturer's directions for packaged popping corn, and go on to step 4, or follow steps 2 and 3.

2. In a 3-quart saucepan heat the oil. Add 2 or 3 of the popcorn kernels. When the kernels pop, add the remaining kernels and cover the pot.

3. Cook over medium heat, shaking the pan often. The popcorn will soon begin to pop. When the popping stops, remove the pan from the heat.

4. Quickly pour the popcorn into a shallow ovenproof serving dish or a baking sheet.

5. Sprinkle the popcorn with the grated cheese, then the chilies, and finally the chili powder.

6. Set the oven to broil (550°F, 288°C).

7. Broil the nachos for 2 to 3 minutes, until the cheese is melted. Serve immediately.

Makes 4 servings.

2 tablespoons vegetable oil

1/4 cup popcorn kernels

1 cup grated cheese

2 tablespoons diced mild green chilies

1 teaspoon chili powder

Popcorn Nachos can also be prepared in the microwave oven. Pour the popped corn into a shallow microwave dish. Assemble as above. Place the dish in the microwave oven and cook on high for 30 to 40 seconds, until the cheese is melted.

PROTEINS

Proteins are a type of molecule found in all animals and plants. Each protein is made from smaller molecules called amino acids. When you eat proteins, your body breaks them apart into amino acids and uses those amino acids to build new proteins that it needs.

In order for amino acids to form a protein, they link together into a long chain, like a line of people holding hands. There are only twenty different amino acids. They are all similar in shape, but each one contains its own unique side chain. It is as though each of the people in the line were wearing one of twenty different hats. An almost endless number of proteins can be formed by making chains of different lengths, each with a different combination of amino acids.

Every protein folds naturally into its own special shape. Some proteins are shaped like springs. Some are shaped like doughnuts. Some look like flat sheets. And some look like tangled balls of yarn. The shape of the protein determines what the protein does inside the plant or animal.

Proteins change dramatically when they are cooked. When proteins come in contact with heat, salt, alcohol, or an acid such as lemon juice, they start to unfold. Once they have lost their natural, folded shape, they are called denatured (unnatural) proteins.

Proteins are found in many foods you eat. Many of these foods are cooked specifically to change the proteins. In the sections that follow, you will see:

- *What happens to egg proteins when they are denatured.*

- *Why milk proteins curdle.*

- *How a protein called collagen is used to make gelatin.*

Why are hard-boiled eggs hard?

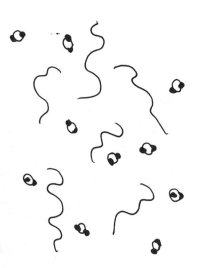

When you boil a liquid, what happens? More than likely it turns into a gas. If you boil it long enough, all the liquid boils away. But raw eggs are a liquid. When you boil them, they become solid! And once solid, they can never turn to liquid again. Why are eggs the exception to the rule?

Eggs are made of proteins, fats, and water. Most of an egg's proteins are shaped like tangled balls of yarn, and are called globular proteins. A raw egg is liquid because the water inside it is able to flow freely between the globular proteins.

When an egg is heated, all the molecules inside it begin to shake. The shaking causes the globular proteins to unwind. They are now in a denatured (unnatural) state. As they unwind, the denatured proteins get tangled with each other.

The water in both the white and the yolk gets trapped in the tangled net of denatured proteins. The egg becomes hard because the water can no longer move around freely.

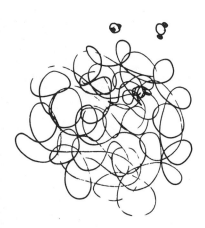

Whole proteins

When making scrambled eggs, if you add milk or water, it also becomes trapped in the protein net. The more the eggs are heated, the more the proteins unwind and become tangled, and the tighter the net becomes. If you overcook the eggs, the net becomes so tight that it starts to squeeze out the water in the milk. You end up with runny eggs.

When making poached eggs, where the raw eggs are cracked and placed gently on the surface of boiling water, most people add vinegar to the water. The vinegar helps denature the proteins on the surface of the eggs and prevents them from falling apart in the hot water before they are cooked through.

When making hard-boiled eggs, you can add salt to the water in order to prevent any egg white from leaking out of a crack in the shell. The salt will denature the leaking proteins even more quickly than the heat of the water, sealing the crack.

Denatured proteins

46

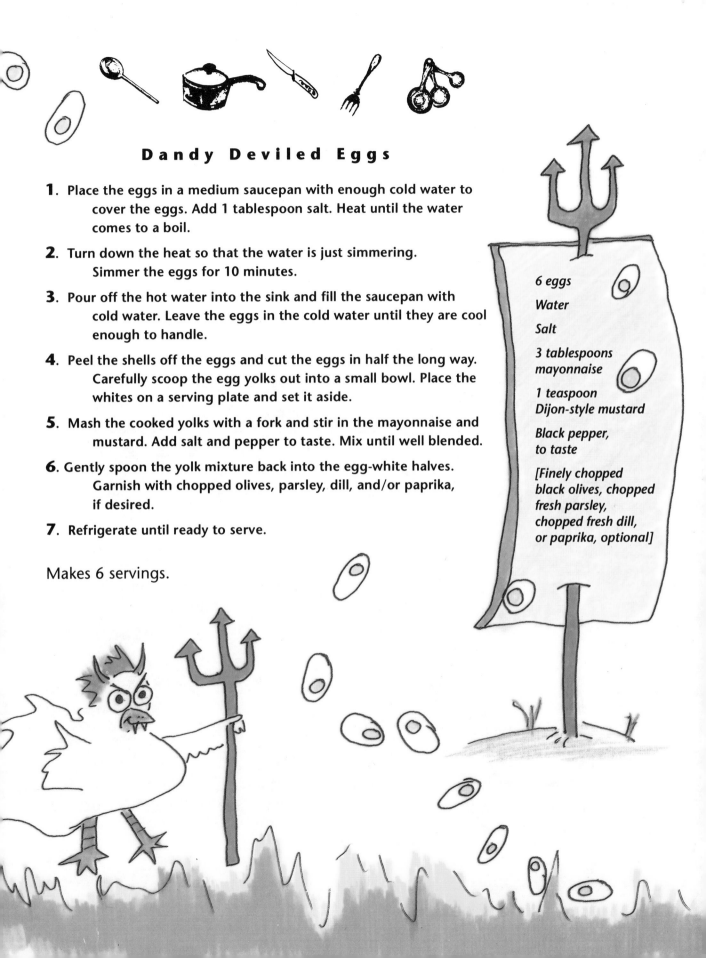

Dandy Deviled Eggs

1. Place the eggs in a medium saucepan with enough cold water to cover the eggs. Add 1 tablespoon salt. Heat until the water comes to a boil.

2. Turn down the heat so that the water is just simmering. Simmer the eggs for 10 minutes.

3. Pour off the hot water into the sink and fill the saucepan with cold water. Leave the eggs in the cold water until they are cool enough to handle.

4. Peel the shells off the eggs and cut the eggs in half the long way. Carefully scoop the egg yolks out into a small bowl. Place the whites on a serving plate and set it aside.

5. Mash the cooked yolks with a fork and stir in the mayonnaise and mustard. Add salt and pepper to taste. Mix until well blended.

6. Gently spoon the yolk mixture back into the egg-white halves. Garnish with chopped olives, parsley, dill, and/or paprika, if desired.

7. Refrigerate until ready to serve.

Makes 6 servings.

6 eggs

Water

Salt

3 tablespoons mayonnaise

1 teaspoon Dijon-style mustard

Black pepper, to taste

[Finely chopped black olives, chopped fresh parsley, chopped fresh dill, or paprika, optional]

What are curds and whey?

In the Mother Goose rhyme, Little Miss Muffet sat on a tuffet, eating her curds and whey. But what *are* curds and whey? Actually, they are very common. They come from milk.

To understand how to make curds and whey, you need to understand the composition of milk. Milk is made up of several things, including fat, water, sugar, protein, and minerals.

The fat in milk is found in small, lumpy globules that float in the water. If you allow milk that's fresh from the cow to stand for a while, the fat globules float to the top and form a layer of cream. That's because the fat is lighter than water.

Most milk that we drink today is homogenized. This means that fresh milk is pumped through a valve at very high pressure to break the fat globules into very tiny balls. The tiny fat balls cannot rise as easily as the larger globules. They do not float to the top. Milk is also pasteurized—heated briefly to a high temperature. The heat kills microbes (germs), making the milk safe to drink and extending its shelf life (amount of time you can store it).

There are two groups of protein in milk, casein (kay-SEEN) and whey. Casein proteins exist naturally in small clusters that gently pull away from each other. These clusters are like tiny sponges that contain large amounts of water.

WHAT'D I DO?

When milk is heated or mixed with salt or acids (such as lemon juice), the denatured casein proteins no longer repel each other. Instead, they clump together and form solid curds. The remaining liquid is called the whey. Curds are mostly protein and fat, while whey is mostly water. If the entire mixture is squeezed through a cheesecloth, the curds that remain in the cloth can be used to make cheese.

Back in Miss Muffet's day, most cheese was made at home. Families made a lot of cheese at a time, because aged cheese can be stored and eaten over many months. The fresh curds and whey Miss Muffet was eating were a special treat eaten at cheese-making time.

You can enjoy fresh cheese, such as cottage cheese or ricotta, anytime. It requires just one step beyond making curds and whey and is very easy.

Ricotta Cheese

1 quart whole or low-fat milk

4 1/2 teaspoons white vinegar

Cheesecloth

1/8 teaspoon salt, or to taste

1. In a medium saucepan, mix the milk and the vinegar.

2. Place the pan over low heat and very slowly bring the mixture to a simmer. The milk will look slightly foamy, and there will be tiny bubbles around the edge.

3. Remove the pan from the heat. Cover it and set it in an enclosed place where it will not be disturbed and where its temperature will stay between 80°F and 100°F (27°-38°C). An unheated oven without a pilot light is fine. Let the milk stand about 6 hours, or until the curds and whey have separated.

4. Line a sieve with a double layer of cheesecloth and set it over a bowl or a 4-cup measuring cup it fits completely into.

5. Pour the curds and whey into the sieve and allow the whey to drain through the cloth and sieve for 1 hour.

6. Turn the cheese out of the cheesecloth into a small bowl. Stir in the salt. Cover and refrigerate 24 hours before serving.

Makes about 3/4 cup.

YOU CAN USE THIS CHEESE WHEN MAKING LASAGNA —OR YOU CAN EAT IT PLAIN.

What is gelatin?

A tiny amount of dry gelatin can turn a large bowl of liquid into a dessert that's wiggly, wet, and weird. Gelatin can also be used to thicken such foods as pies and marshmallows. What is gelatin and how does it work?

Gelatin is made from a unique protein called collagen that is found in your body and the bodies of most animals. Collagen is made of three separate chains of amino acids, the building blocks of proteins. The chains are like strands of rope twisted together. The three amino acid chains are held together by weak bonds. But overall, the collagen is very strong and forms the connective tissue that holds our bodies together.

When making gelatin, a manufacturer heats animal collagen to a very high temperature. Most of the weak bonds between the amino acid chains break. The denatured protein that results is then known as gelatin. You can make your own gelatin from meat bones by boiling some that have connective tissue on them. If you cool the broth you have made from them in a refrigerator overnight, it will not be liquid. It will be a gel.

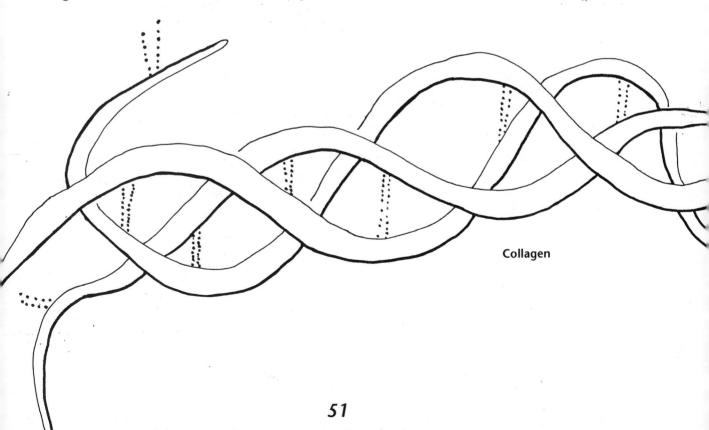

Collagen

When you use dry packaged gelatin in cooking, you add it to cold water. The cold water softens and spreads out the gelatin so that it does not clump together. Next, you heat the gelatin and water to dissolve the gelatin. After the gelatin is dissolved, you add the other ingredients. Then you refrigerate the whole mixture.

As the gelatin cools, the long amino acid chains form weak bonds again. But because the gelatin is mixed with other ingredients, it does not form the original bonds. It forms a big net that traps the liquid in the mixture. The more the gelatin cools, the more those bonds form and the more solid the mixture becomes.

Even in small amounts, gelatin is extremely good at turning liquids into solids. You can see how it works by making the marshmallows in the following recipe.

Is a gel a solid or a liquid? It is actually both. A gel contains a liquid trapped in a solid. That is what makes it wiggly.

Fresh pineapple contains an enzyme called bromelain that chops collagen into tiny pieces. So if you use fresh pineapple in gelatin, it won't gel. In canned pineapple the bromelain has been destroyed and won't hurt your gelatin.

Magic Marshmallows

1. In a small bowl, mix the confectioners' sugar and the cornstarch.

2. Lightly butter the bottom and sides of an 8- or 9-inch-square pan. Cut a piece of waxed paper to fit the bottom of the pan. Place it in the pan and grease the top of the paper.

3. Dust the bottom and sides of the pan well with some of the sugar-cornstarch mixture.

4. In a small saucepan, mix the unflavored gelatin and the water. Let stand for 1 minute.

5. Cook and stir over medium heat until the gelatin completely dissolves, about 1 minute.

6. Pour the gelatin mixture into a large bowl. Add the granulated sugar, corn syrup, and vanilla.

7. Beat with an electric mixer at high speed for 15 minutes, until the mixture becomes very thick and creamy.

8. Pour the mixture into the prepared pan. Spread it evenly in the pan. Let it stand at room temperature for 4 hours or overnight.

9. Dust a cutting board with the remaining cornstarch mixture. Loosen the sides of the marshmallows from the pan with a sharp knife. Carefully turn out onto the coated board.

10. Dip the knife into hot water and cut the marshmallows into 1-inch cubes. (Keeping the knife wet prevents the marshmallows from sticking to it.)

11. Roll the cubes in the cornstarch mixture until they are well coated.

12. Let the marshmallows air-dry for several hours, then store in an airtight container.

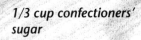

1/3 cup confectioners' sugar

1/3 cup cornstarch

Butter or margarine for greasing pan

2 envelopes unflavored gelatin

1/2 cup cold water

1/2 cup granulated sugar

1 cup light corn syrup

1 teaspoon vanilla

Makes about 80 marshmallows.

You can color your marshmallows by adding food coloring, a drop at a time, while beating the marshmallow mixture (step 7), until the mixture is the shade you like. You can also add some flavoring, to taste, such as peppermint oil, cinnamon oil, or lemon extract.

CELLS

All living things are made of cells, which you can see only through a microscope. Cells are like tiny factories, each of which is designed to perform a specific task. The shape and size of each cell is determined by the task it performs.

Animal cells are like tiny bubbles filled with salty water. They have many specialized parts. The outside skin of each cell, called the membrane, is made of two layers of fat molecules.

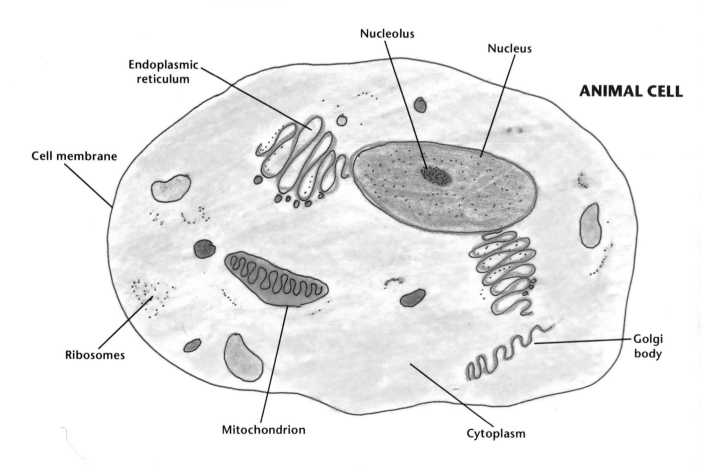

Nucleolus

Nucleus

Endoplasmic reticulum

ANIMAL CELL

Cell membrane

Ribosomes

Golgi body

Mitochondrion

Cytoplasm

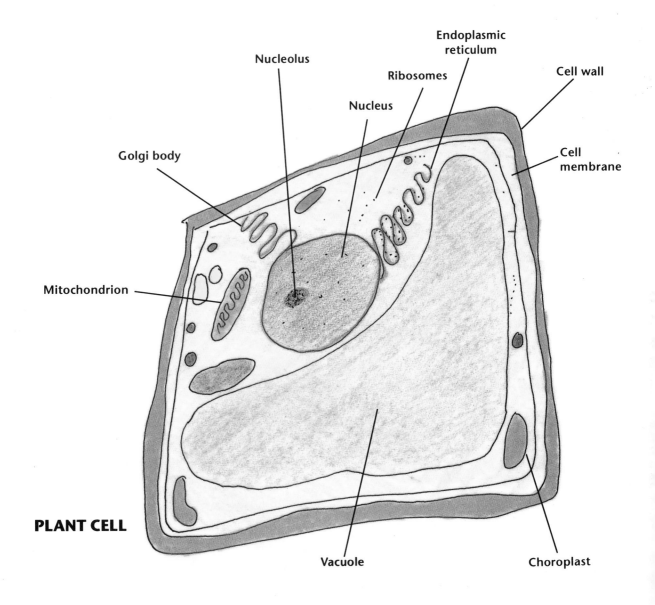

Golgi body

Nucleolus

Nucleus

Ribosomes

Endoplasmic reticulum

Cell wall

Cell membrane

Mitochondrion

PLANT CELL

Vacuole

Choroplast

Plant cells are somewhat different because they have an additional type of membrane around them, called a cell wall. The cell wall is much stronger than the cell membrane in animals. It helps plants withstand such forces of nature as strong winds and invading microbes. It gives some raw vegetables their crunch. In addition, a plant cell contains a large sac called a vacuole, which stores water.

Fungus cells are different from both plant and animal cells. Unlike plants, funguses do not make their own food. Funguses range from yeast, a single cell, to mushrooms.

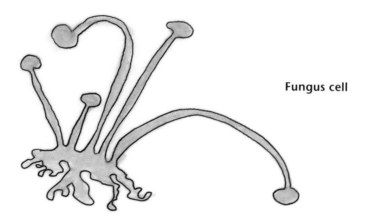

Fungus cell

Protists and monera also have only one cell. These tiny living things can be found in pond water, on your skin, in the food you eat—almost everywhere. But they are so tiny that you can see them only under a microscope.

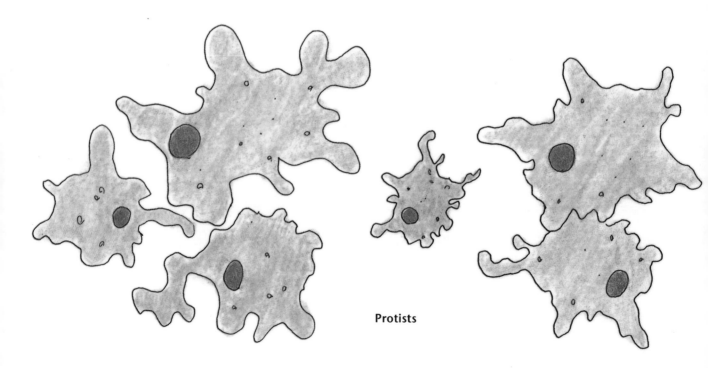

Protists

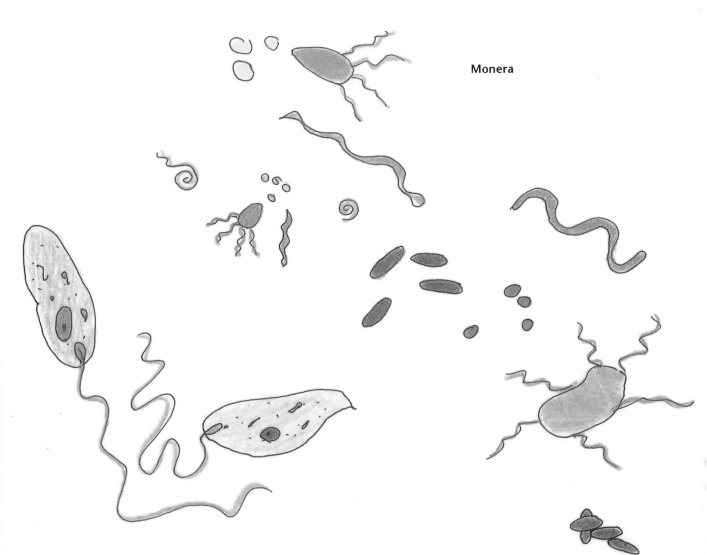

Monera

In the following sections, you will read about different types of cells. You will discover:

- *Why some plants wilt when they are cooked.*

- *How onions protect themselves from being eaten.*

- *How certain cells make bread rise.*

- *How cells create yogurt.*

- *How the light and the dark meat of a chicken differ, and why the differences are just as important to a chicken as to a cook.*

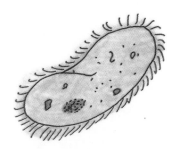

Why do some fruits and vegetables wilt when cooked?

Have you ever noticed that when you cook many fruits and vegetables, their texture changes from firm and crisp to limp and soft? Why does this happen?

The strong cell walls of a plant are made of cellulose, which forms the cell's framework. If the vacuole (sac) of each plant cell is filled with water, the plant is firm and rigid. When the sac is not full, the plant cells are limp and the leaves droop.

When you cook fruits and vegetables, the heat causes the cell walls to weaken, and the water to leak out of the cell. The plant becomes wilted and limp.

Some fruits and vegetables are more sensitive to heat than others. That depends on the strength of the cell walls, the amount of water in the cells, and the thickness of the plant part being used. Carrot (root) cells, for example, contain less water and have much stronger cell walls than do spinach (leaf) cells. As a result, carrots do not wilt as quickly as spinach when they are cooked. You can see the effect of heat on apples when you make the following recipe for apple crisp.

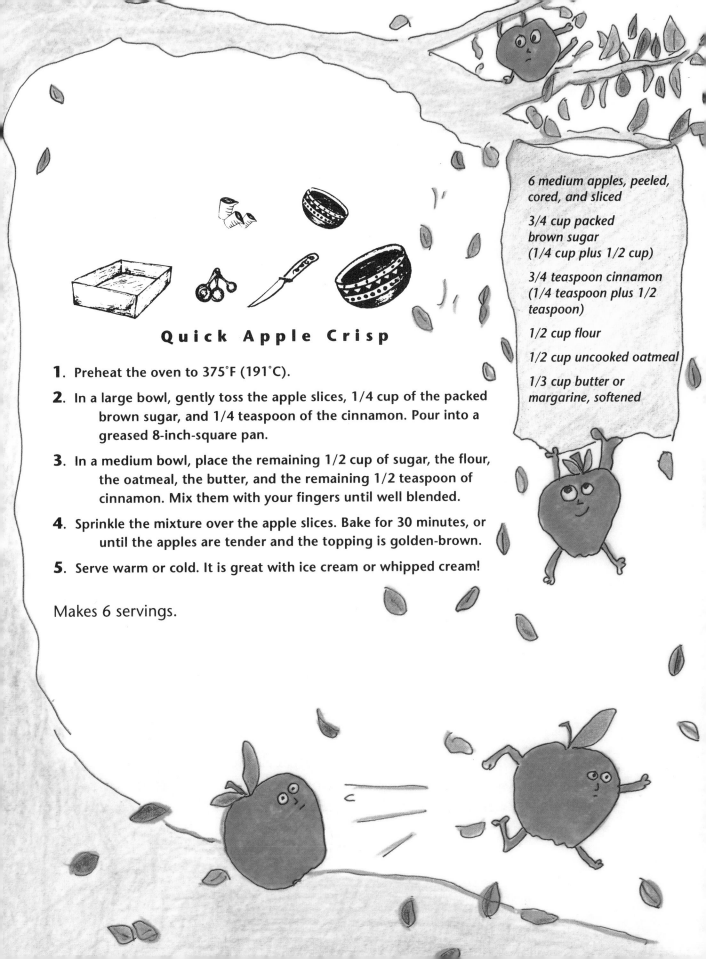

Quick Apple Crisp

6 medium apples, peeled, cored, and sliced

3/4 cup packed brown sugar (1/4 cup plus 1/2 cup)

3/4 teaspoon cinnamon (1/4 teaspoon plus 1/2 teaspoon)

1/2 cup flour

1/2 cup uncooked oatmeal

1/3 cup butter or margarine, softened

1. Preheat the oven to 375°F (191°C).

2. In a large bowl, gently toss the apple slices, 1/4 cup of the packed brown sugar, and 1/4 teaspoon of the cinnamon. Pour into a greased 8-inch-square pan.

3. In a medium bowl, place the remaining 1/2 cup of sugar, the flour, the oatmeal, the butter, and the remaining 1/2 teaspoon of cinnamon. Mix them with your fingers until well blended.

4. Sprinkle the mixture over the apple slices. Bake for 30 minutes, or until the apples are tender and the topping is golden-brown.

5. Serve warm or cold. It is great with ice cream or whipped cream!

Makes 6 servings.

Why do onions make you cry?

Have you ever cut an onion? How long does it take until your eyes start to burn and tears begin running down your face? If you never want onions to make you cry again, you can find out how it happens and how to prevent it.

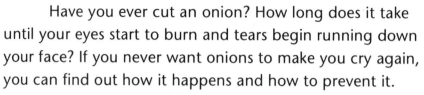

Like other plants, onions are made up of cells. Onions cells have a special molecule that contains the chemical element sulfur. Between the cells is another molecule, called an enzyme, that speeds up chemical reactions. The sulfur-containing molecules and the enzymes sit quietly on opposite sides of cell wall—until the cells are cut open.

Then the sulfur-containing molecules and the enzymes come into contact and start a chain of chemical reactions. You cannot see these reactions, but you can feel the results. New molecules are released, float up into the air, and sting your eyes. Since the new molecules contain sulfur, when they react with the tears in your eyes, they form sulfuric acid. No wonder they burn!

CRYBABY!

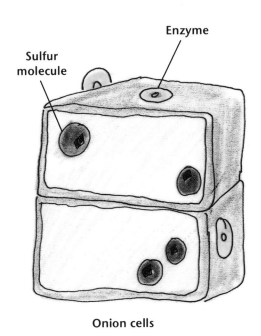

Sulfur molecule

Enzyme

Onion cells

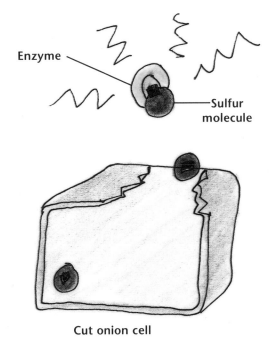

Enzyme

Sulfur molecule

Cut onion cell

   The strong-smelling molecules in onions and garlic protect the plants from being eaten by small animals and bugs. People have learned to enjoy the flavor of these molecules in small amounts.

   When you cook an onion, the molecules inside the onion cells are changed. They smell and taste much sweeter than raw onions too, and will not make you cry when they are cut.

   Now that you know what causes onions to make you cry, there are things you can do to prevent it. As you cut an onion, you can put it under cold water. The burning molecules will react with the water before they get to your eyes. Or you can put the onion in the freezer 10 to 15 minutes before you cut it open. The reaction that takes place in the onion is slowed down by low temperatures, and fewer of the burning molecules will be formed.

   When you prepare the onion soup that follows, which method will you choose to avoid having the onions make you cry?

French Onion Soup

3 large onions, sliced thin (about 4 cups)

4 tablespoons margarine or butter

3 cans (13 3/4 ounces each) beef broth

6 slices French bread, toasted

1 1/2 cups (6 ounces) shredded Swiss or Gruyère cheese

(You can use up to 12 ounces of cheese if you like.)

1. In a large pot over medium heat, cook onions in margarine, stirring occasionally, until onions are tender and start to brown.

2. Gradually stir in 1 can of the broth.

3. Heat to a boil, stirring constantly.

4. Stir in the rest of the broth and heat to a boil.

5. Reduce heat and simmer for 5 minutes.

6. Place 1 slice toast in each of 6 ovenproof soup bowls. (If you don't have these, you can finish preparing the soup in a large ovenproof casserole and spoon it into separate bowls after it is finished.)

7. Pour an equal amount of soup over toast in each bowl and sprinkle with equal amounts of cheese.

8. Set oven control to broil (550°F, 288°C).

9. Place tops of bowls 3-4 inches from heat and broil until cheese is melted and light brown, about 3 minutes. (If you have used more cheese, it will take a little longer.)

10. Be very careful when removing these very hot bowls from the oven. Use ovenproof mitts or pot holders. Let the soup cool off a bit so you don't burn your mouth when you eat it.

Makes 6 servings.

What is the difference between light and dark meat?

People eat the meat of many different animals, including chickens, cows, and fish. Most of the meat they eat comes from the animal's muscles. Some muscles are lighter in color and some are darker. Why?

If you look at different muscles under a microscope, you can see two types of muscle cells: white and red. Light meat has more white muscle cells. Dark meat has more red muscle cells.

Red muscle cells are designed to stay active for long periods of time. They are found in the legs of animals that run for long distances and in the wings of animals that fly for long periods of time. In order to maintain that activity, red muscle cells need energy. The source of the energy is fat, which is located in and around red muscle cells. In order to burn fat, these cells need oxygen. A special molecule called myoglobin stores oxygen in red muscle cells. It is bright red. This is why very active muscles are dark in color.

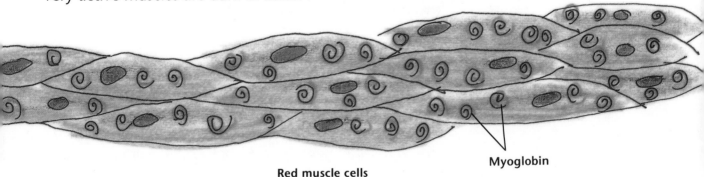

Red muscle cells

Myoglobin

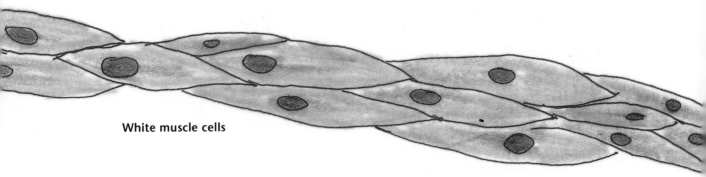

White muscle cells

White muscle cells are found in muscles that are needed for only short bursts of activity, such as those in the breast and the wings of a chicken. These muscles can rely on the limited amount of sugar that circulates in the blood as a source of energy. As a result, these muscles do not have much fat. Since sugar can be burned without oxygen, these molecules do not have any need for myoglobin. These cells are light in color.

Fish have mostly white muscle cells. That's because fish float in the water and need only a small amount of energy to move around. Ducks, however, must work very hard for long periods of time when they are flying. As a result, the muscles in their wings and their breasts are composed mostly of red muscle cells.

Light meat and dark meat taste different from each other. Which one do you like best? Here's a recipe that can use either one—or both.

Thai Chicken Kabobs

1. In a medium bowl or plastic container with a watertight lid, blend the peanut butter, honey, soy sauce, water, ginger, and red pepper.

2. Add the chicken pieces and mix well. Cover and marinate in the refrigerator for at least 2 hours, stirring occasionally. (If the chicken is in a plastic container, turn the container over occasionally to mix ingredients.)

3. Preheat the oven to 425°F (218°C).

4. Cover a baking sheet with aluminum foil. Thread the chicken pieces onto the skewers, leaving spaces between the chicken pieces. Place the skewers on the baking sheet.

5. Bake 10 minutes. Turn the chicken skewers over and bake for 10 minutes longer, until the chicken is tender.

6. Remove from the oven and serve hot.

Makes 4 servings.

3 tablespoons creamy peanut butter

3 tablespoons honey

2 tablespoons soy sauce

1 tablespoon water

1/4 teaspoon ground ginger

Dash of ground red pepper (cayenne)

About 1 1/4 pounds boneless chicken breasts or thighs or a combination of both, cut into 1 1/2-inch squares

Wooden skewers

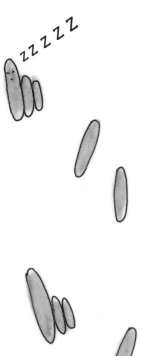

Why does yeast make bread rise?

There is something almost magical in the way bread rises. But it isn't really magic. It's yeast and gluten. What are they, and how do they make bread rise?

Yeast is a kind of microbe, a living thing that can be seen only under a microscope. It is made up of just one cell and belongs to the fungus family (which includes mushrooms). Yeast can be stored in an inactive state for long periods of time in packets in your refrigerator. When it is added to warm, moist bread dough, it comes back to life. The yeast eats the starch in the dough, which gives the yeast energy to reproduce.

While digesting the starch, yeast gives off carbon dioxide gas and alcohol as waste products. The alcohol evaporates into the air, and the carbon dioxide gas becomes trapped as bubbles in the dough. The gas bubbles are trapped because the dough contains gluten. Gluten is a tangled net of protein that is formed when water is added to flour. Gluten is stretchy, like bubble gum, and can contain the expanding gas. The more the dough is kneaded, the more gluten is formed.

As the yeast consumes the starch in the dough, it produces more and more carbon dioxide gas. The gas pockets expand, causing the dough to rise. You then "punch" down the dough to collapse many of the gas bubbles. If you let the dough rise too long, the yeast will be killed by the gas, its own waste. But the dough can be allowed to rise again and then punched down any number of times before it is shaped into a loaf. The number of risings changes the texture of the bread.

Traditional bread loaves are allowed to rise twice before they are put into a hot oven. Other risen products, such as pretzels and pizza dough, are put into the oven with only one rising. In the oven, the dough gets very hot, the yeast dies, and no more carbon dioxide gas is produced.

The gas *already* in the bread dough continues to expand—all gases expand when they are heated—and the loaf continues to grow.

When the outside of the loaf gets hard and crusty, and the loaf cannot expand anymore, the bread is done. It is then allowed to cool as the gas seeps into the air. It leaves behind the tiny holes you see when you look at a slice of bread.

The key to making yeast bread is to provide a comfortable place for the yeast to grow. It needs a wet, warm environment and plenty of food. Warm water provides the moisture, and sugars derived from the starch in the flour serve as the food. With these simple ingredients, yeast helps you to transform a lump of dough into homemade bread.

Baking your own yeast bread can be fun. Making your own pizza is another way to use yeast that's sure to be a crowd pleaser.

Pretty Perfect Pizza

1 cup warm water (about 105˚F to 115˚F, 41˚C to 46˚C—water should feel comfortably warm when sprinkled on the inside of your wrist)

1 envelope active dry yeast

2 tablespoons vegetable oil

1 teaspoon salt

About 3 cups flour

2/3 cup pizza or spaghetti sauce

1 1/3 cups shredded mozzarella cheese

[Sliced mushrooms, green pepper, pepperoni, etc., optional]

1. In a large bowl, combine the water and the yeast. Let them stand for 5 minutes.

2. Stir in the oil and salt. With a wooden spoon, stir in the flour, a cup at a time, until the dough forms a ball that leaves the sides of the bowl.

3. Turn the dough out onto a floured surface and knead it for 8 to 10 minutes, adding flour as needed to prevent the dough from sticking to your hands and to the work surface. The dough is kneaded enough when it feels smooth and elastic. When you press it lightly with your finger, it should spring back, leaving only a slight dent.

4. Shape the dough into a smooth ball and place it in a lightly greased bowl, turning the dough until it is coated with oil. Cover the bowl with plastic wrap.

5. Let the dough rise in a warm, draft-free place for about 1 hour, until it has doubled in size.

6. Punch down the dough with your fist. Knead it for a minute or two until it is very smooth. Let the dough rest for 5 minutes.

7. Preheat the oven to 450°F (232°C).

8. Lightly grease a 12-inch pizza pan or a 13 X 9 X 2-inch baking pan.

9. Roll out the dough with a rolling pin into as large a circle as possible. Then stretch the dough with your fingers until it fits the pan.

10. Spread the sauce over the surface of the dough. Bake on the lower oven shelf for 25 minutes.

11. Remove the pan from the oven and cover the sauce with the cheese. Top with mushrooms, green peppers, or whatever you like on your pizza. Return the pizza to the oven and bake 10 minutes longer, until the cheese is melted.

Makes one pizza.

How to knead dough

Sprinkle a little of the flour from the recipe on a clean work surface. Rub a little flour on your hands. Turn the dough out onto the floured surface. Fold it toward you with your fingers. Push the dough down with the heel of your hands. Give the dough a quarter turn, and repeat the fold and the push. Continue turning, folding, and pushing until the desired consistency is reached, adding flour to the work surface and your hands anytime the dough starts to stick.

What is yogurt?

Bacteria are one-celled microbes even tinier than yeast. When two types of bacteria—*Lactobacillus bulgaricus* and *Streptococcus thermophilus*—are added to milk, the texture and flavor of the milk changes. It becomes yogurt. How does this happen?

Like yeast, bacteria like to eat sugar. The kind of bacteria found in yogurt eat only lactose, a sugar naturally found in milk. When they eat the sugar, they release lactic acid, which makes the milk taste sour. Also, a substance called an aldehyde is formed, which gives yogurt its special flavor.

When the amount of acid in the milk gets high enough, the milk proteins clump together and form lumpy curds. (See the section on curds and whey for more information.) Since the enclosed whey cannot move around in the solution as much as it did in the fresh milk, yogurt is thicker than milk.

70

Lactobacillus
bulgaricus

Streptococcus
thermophilus

IT'S ALIVE!

Yogurt is very easy to make at home. All you need is milk and special lactic-acid bacteria. You can get the bacteria from store-bought yogurt that contains active cultures. (Check the manufacturer's label. Not all yogurt contains active bacteria.)

Temperature control is important to yogurt making. If the temperature gets too high, the bacteria will die. On the other hand, lowering the temperature too much, by placing the yogurt in the refrigerator, stops lactic-acid production altogether. (This is why you store yogurt there.) But if the yogurt is warmed, the bacteria will start reproducing again.

You can make yogurt in a commercial yogurt maker, in your oven, or even in a thermos!

The curds and whey in yogurt are very delicate and can separate if the yogurt is stirred too much or if it is heated to high temperatures. For example, if you stir a container of yogurt and then put it back into the refrigerator, a day later you will find that there is a watery layer on the top. This liquid is whey that has been squeezed out of the curds, just as water is squeezed out of a sponge. If you stir the yogurt to mix the curds and whey, the yogurt will be thinner than it was originally, but it will taste the same.

Although the first commercial yogurt company was founded in Spain in 1919, people have been eating yogurt for thousands of years in Asia and the Middle East. Goat's milk, sheep's milk, and yak's milk are used in various places. People in the mountains of Armenia and Georgia (formerly parts of the Soviet Union near Turkey) eat lots of yogurt.

Homemade Yogurt

2 cups whole or low-fat milk

2 tablespoons plain yogurt with active cultures

3 tablespoons nonfat dry milk

1. In a 1-quart saucepan, heat the milk until it is 100°F to 115°F (38°C to 46°C). (The milk will feel comfortably warm when sprinkled on the inside of your wrist.)

2. Stir in the yogurt and the dry milk until well blended.

3. Put the mixture in a warm place for 4 to 6 hours until the yogurt is thick. For this you can use a commercial yogurt maker (follow the manufacturer's instructions); place the pan in a 100°F (38°C) oven (see Note A); or pour the mixture into a prewarmed thermos (see Note B).

4. Refrigerate the yogurt for several hours. It will thicken as it cools.

5. Serve the yogurt plain, add fruit to it, or mix it with herbs to make a salad dressing.

Makes about 2 cups.

Note A: Since ovens don't have a temperature setting as low as 100°F (38°C), it is necessary to use an oven thermometer that registers as low as 100°F. Turn the oven on to the lowest setting. When the oven thermometer registers 100°F, turn the oven off. It may be necessary to repeat this procedure every hour or so. Do not let the oven temperature get higher than 115°F (46°C). You might kill the lactic-acid bacteria.

Note B: To prewarm the thermos container, fill it with boiling water. Let it stand a couple of minutes. Pour off the water. Then fill the thermos with the warm milk mixture. Cover and set it where it will not be disturbed. Rewarm the thermos in the sink every 2 to 3 hours by pouring boiling water around the outside of the thermos. Return it to its undisturbed place between warmings.

GLOSSARY

ACID See pH.

ALCOHOL In bread making, a waste product that yeast gives off.

AMINO ACID Any of the 20 basic building blocks of proteins. A chain of amino acids forms a protein.

ATMOSPHERIC PRESSURE The push downward on Earth and all objects on Earth by the weight of the air in the atmosphere.

ATOM The smallest particle of any chemical element that can exist either alone or together with other atoms.

BACTERIA Microscopic one-celled creatures that multiply very quickly. They live in air, soil, water, animals, plants, and remains of living things.

BASE See pH.

BOILING The change of a liquid to a gas at a specific temperature, which is called the boiling point.

BOND The strong attraction that holds together atoms in a molecule and molecules in a compound.

CARBOHYDRATE A group of molecules made of carbon, hydrogen, and oxygen, that includes sugars, starches, and cellulose.

CARBON DIOXIDE A colorless gas made of carbon and oxygen. Animals breathe out carbon dioxide and plants breathe it in.

CASEIN A kind of protein found in milk that clumps together when exposed to acid, salt, or high temperatures.

CELL The most basic unit of all living things able to function by itself.

CELLULOSE A long sugar molecule, similar to starch, that gives a plant cell a strong structure.

CELL WALL The strong cell membrane that surrounds individual plant cells.

CHEMICAL REACTION The way in which chemicals combine.

CHEMICAL RELATIONSHIP A permanent bond that exists between the atoms and molecules of different substances, such as when you mix salt and water.

COLLAGEN A very strong protein found in animals that is used to make gelatin.

COMPOUND A substance made up of more than one kind of atom. Examples include water, alcohol, fat, sugar, and starch.

CRYSTAL A solid in which the atoms line up in the same geometric pattern over and over again.

CURD The thick, lumpy part of milk that has been exposed to acid, heat, or high temperatures.

DENATURING The destruction of the original properties of a molecule.

ELEMENT One of about a hundred substances that consist of only one kind of atom and that by themselves or in combination make up all matter.

EMULSIFIER A substance that contains a "water-loving" molecule on one end and a "water-fearing" molecule on the other end. Its presence allows you to mix substances such as oil and water that you can't usually mix.

ENERGY The ability to do work. There are several forms of energy, including heat, electrical, and mechanical energy.

ENZYME A protein that speeds up a specific chemical reaction.

EVAPORATION The slow change of a liquid into a gas, such as water into vapor.

FAT A kind of molecule that is stored by animals and plants as an important source of energy.

FREEZING The change of a liquid to a solid at a specific temperature, the freezing point. This is the same temperature as the melting point.

GAS A state of matter in which the particles are far apart, move freely inside a container, and fill any space available.

GELATIN Collagen that has been denatured by boiling. Gelatin is used to create a gel, a solid with a liquid trapped inside.

GLOSSARY

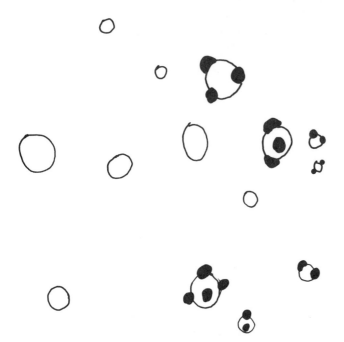

Microbe A tiny living thing so small that it can be seen only under a microscope. Examples of microbes include bacteria and yeast.

Molecule The smallest particle of a substance that has the properties of that substance. A molecule is made up of atoms.

Myoglobin A large protein found in red muscle cells that holds oxygen from the blood for later use by active muscles.

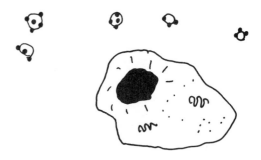

Gluten A rubbery mixture of wheat protein and water, formed when bread dough is kneaded. Gluten helps contain the carbon dioxide gas produced by yeast in bread making.

Homogenization The process of creating a solution that is the same all over. Milk is homogenized by breaking the fat globules into tiny balls so they do not rise to the surface of the milk.

Liquid A state of matter in which the volume of a substance stays the same but the shape depends on the shape of the container it is in.

Matter Matter is something that has weight and takes up space. Matter exists in one of three states: solid, liquid, and gas.

Melting The change of a solid into a liquid at a specific temperature, which is called the melting point. This is the same temperature as the freezing point.

Nucleus The part of animal and plant cells where instructions are given for cell functions and making new cells.

Oil A fat that is a liquid at room temperature.

PASTEURIZATION The process of heating a substance, such as milk, to a high temperature to kill unwanted microbes.

pH A measure of how acidic (sour) or basic (bitter) a solution is. A pH equal to 7.0 is neutral (neither acidic nor basic). A pH below 7.0 is an acid, and a pH above 7.0 is a base.

PIGMENT A type of molecule that gives color to a substance.

PROTEIN One of the most common kinds of molecules in living things. They are made up of one or more chains of amino acids.

RED MUSCLE CELLS Muscle cells found mainly in the legs and wings of animals that run and fly long distances. These cells can be active for long periods of time.

SOLID A substance that has a definite shape.

SOLUTION A mixture in which one or more ingredients dissolves in a liquid.

STARCH A long molecule made of a chain of sugar molecules bonded together.

SUGAR Any of a group of sweet-tasting carbohydrates.

VAPOR PRESSURE The upward pressure from liquid molecules that have turned to a gas. As the temperature rises (as in boiling) the vapor pressure increases.

WHEY The watery portion of milk that remains when the casein proteins are curdled by acid or salt.

WHITE MUSCLE CELLS Muscle cells that are very active for brief periods of time and use blood sugar as a source of energy.

YEAST A type of one-celled microbe used to help bread dough rise.

INDEX

There are several people I would like to thank for helping to make this book possible. First is my editor, Marc Gave, who expertly managed this project. Next is Lucy Holtzman Gave, who tested all of the recipes and made delicious suggestions. I would also like to acknowledge Dick Kleyn and Lucy Williams, for their technical comments on the manuscript, and Bo Park, for her comments based on teaching food chemistry to kids.

THE END